You can KNIT!

Knit and purl your way through 12 fun and easy projects

Stephanie White

Fons&Porter

CINCINNATI, OHIO

contents

Introduction 4

What is Knitting? 6

How to Use This Book . . . 6

Tools + Materials 8

1

garter stitch

10

2

stockinette stitch

42

3

ribbing

68

4

seed stitch

94

Common Mistakes . . 120

Index 125

About the Author . . . 126

Introduction

Look, I'm not going to waste your time telling you how easy knitting is and that it's something blindfolded babies can do. Of course I think it's easy; I've been knitting for the last twenty years. The important thing to take away from this introduction is that you can knit. I really mean that. Some people may take longer than others to get the hang of it, but at the end of the day, it is a skill you can master. Or, if not master, at least do passably well.

In writing this book, my goal was to make you feel like I'm sitting right beside you every step of the way. Unlike other beginning knitting books, I'm not just going to show you the basics and cut you lose; I will show you the basics, then show you exactly how those basics make the projects in this book. Yes, you may still run into trouble. At that point, you should flip to the Common Mistakes section at the end of the book. But really, at this stage in the knitting game, the best way to fix a mistake is to rip it out and start over. Once you've done that once or twice, you'll realize that making mistakes isn't so scary, because you've already experienced the worst that can happen (*starting over*) and come through it a better knitter.

There's a little bit of info you need to know before you get started, so scan the next few pages, then turn to Chapter One and learn how to knit. You've got this.

What is Knitting?

At its most fundamental, knitting is just a series of interconnected loops. Each time you knit a stitch, you're pulling a new loop through an existing loop. In the knitting world, we don't refer to them as loops. We call them stitches, but they really are just loops.

There are two types of stitches you can make: a knit stitch and a purl stitch. Both of these stitches are just loops. The only difference is how you pull the loop through the stitch below. This will make a lot more sense once you actually start knitting.

All of the projects in this book are combinations of knit and purl stitches. When you learn a new stitch pattern (confusingly also referred to as a stitch), you're just learning a new way to combine knit and purl stitches. To make the garter stitch, you only need to know the knit stitch. Stockinette stitch is also just a stitch pattern that uses knits and purls. Again, all of this will become clear as you start working on your projects.

Another confusing bit worth mentioning is the term "knit." People use it to refer to both the specific knit stitch and the activity itself, encompassing all the various stitches, stitch patterns, etc. When writing the instructions for this book, I tried to use the word *knit* only when you actively need to knit a stitch, not purl a stitch, nor when you work a pattern stitch. Hopefully this will help lessen any confusion.

How to Use This Book

This book assumes you've never knit before, or if you have, you really don't remember how you did it. There are four chapters, with each chapter building on the previous chapter. Within each chapter are three coordinating projects, all using the same needle size, type of yarn and stitch pattern.

Each chapter begins with a gauge swatch tutorial. Knitting a gauge swatch is a step that many knitters skip, but it really makes a difference to your finished projects. Every pattern calls for a specific gauge: So many stitches over so many rows equals a certain measurement. Your knitting needs to come out to that same measurement in order for your finished project to be the right size.

Full disclosure: Getting your gauge exactly right isn't crucial for the projects in this book. In fact, don't worry about the row gauge at all. The patterns almost always tell you to knit to a certain length, so if it takes you more or fewer rows of knitting to get there, it's no big deal. As for making sure you have the right number of stitches per inch (2.5cm), as long as you're close, it should be okay. These projects are forgiving, so if you're off slightly, don't worry about it.

That being said, it's still important to knit the swatches. Each swatch in this book serves as a practice project, introducing you to the techniques you'll need to finish the other projects in the chapter. When you're done with the swatch, you'll turn it into a mug mat or coaster. That way it's practice you can use.

If you're slightly more familiar with knitting, you can skip through the step-by-step photos and head straight to the end of each project. There you'll find the straightforward, no-frills knitting pattern. Beginning knitters should look at the patterns from time to time, too. It's helpful to see how all the work you're doing translates into a pattern.

Another fun bonus: Each project calls for yarn individually. However, at the beginning of each chapter, you can see how much yarn you'll need if you want to knit all of the projects in a chapter (usually a lot less than if you just add up the yarn called for in each individual project). Knit all the projects. Make yourself coordinated accessories. You won't regret it.

And there you have it. Start with the first chapter, knit up your gauge swatch, then dive into the projects. If you want to skip around a bit, that's fine. You can always flip back to an earlier chapter's gauge swatch to brush up on a few techniques if you need to.

Tools + Materials

CHOOSING YARN

Choosing yarn was my favorite part of writing this book. There are so many colors, textures and materials to choose from. Sometimes this can be a bit overwhelming, and for that reason, I've told you exactly which yarns I've used for each project, in case you want a no-brainer option.

If you're choosing your own yarns, the first thing you need to be aware of is the weight of your yarn. The projects in this book use three different weights: super bulky, bulky and medium weight. Super bulky is the heaviest of the three; it's great for knitting projects fast. Bulky yarn is slightly less thick and dense, but is still great for quick knitting. Medium is the thinnest of the three, but it's a very popular weight, so you'll have tons of options when you're looking for yarn. There are other weights, smaller than these three, but we won't use them in this book.

To determine what weight a yarn is, look at the label. You'll find a picture of a skein (or ball) of yarn with a number on it: 4 is medium, 5 is bulky and 6 is super bulky. When choosing yarn for these projects, make sure you choose a yarn that is the same weight as the original project.

Once you've narrowed down the right weight, you'll have to decide what type of fiber you want. Wool is a classic, but it can sometimes be itchy (depending on the type of wool). Acrylic yarns are cheaper and stand up to almost anything, but they may not look or feel as nice as you'd like. I tend to go for wool/acrylic blends. They have a little bit of the fuzziness of a wool yarn, but they aren't quite as warm and don't tend to be scratchy.

Really, you can choose anything you like the look and feel of, though I do recommend staying away from cotton yarns for these projects; they don't have enough stretch. I also advise that you avoid excessively fuzzy yarns at first. With so much extra fuzz, it can be difficult to get your needles through the stitches.

SUPER BULKY

BULKY

MEDIUM

KNITTING NEEDLES

Like yarn, knitting needles are made in a variety of materials, including bamboo, aluminium and plastic. No one needle is better than another, so choose what feels right to you. I prefer working with bamboo or other wooden needles because, to me, they have just the right balance of holding my yarn on the needle. Aluminium needles can be a bit slippery, which is good if you're a tight knitter. Personally, I don't like the clank of aluminium needles hitting one another, but to each her own.

Knitting needles come in different sizes, indicated by a number. The higher the number, the bigger the needle. At the beginning of each chapter, I'll tell you what size needles to use. You'll use those same needles for the entire chapter. There are three different needle sizes used in the book (US 8 [5mm], 9 [5.5mm] and 10 [6mm]), but you may also want to grab a pair of US 7 [4.5mm] and 10½ [6.5mm] just to have them on hand. If it turns out you knit with a different tension than I do, you may need to change your needle size.

OTHER SUPPLIES

Aside from yarn and needles, there are only a few other essentials you need before you get started. A **tape measure** is crucial. Use a cloth tape if you have one. It will make things like measuring the circumference of your head much easier.

You'll also need a sharp pair of **scissors**. I use a small pair so I can take them with me when I'm knitting on the go. They don't have to be anything special, but do make sure you have some. I don't recommend trying to break yarn with your hands.

The last essential is a **yarn needle**. This needle looks like a sewing needle, but it has a large eye and a blunt tip, which makes it perfect for weaving in ends. These needles come with either straight or angled tips. Choose whichever you prefer.

Once you've gathered these supplies, you can make any of the projects in this book.

One optional tool: I personally believe everything is better if you put a pom-pom on it. If you also share this sentiment, I suggest you invest in a pom-pom maker. You can make pom-poms without one, but it definitely speeds up the process.

1
garter stitch

The simplest of all stitch patterns, garter stitch, is also my favorite. I love the graphic, ridged pattern it creates, and I love that I never have to worry about the edges curling. Garter stitch lies flat.

The projects in this chapter are the easiest projects in the book (all knit stitches, no purls!), but the addition of pom-poms and playful color choices make them stylish and fun.

FOR THESE PROJECTS

If you plan on knitting all the projects in this chapter, you need the following:

- **2 skeins of super bulky yarn in teal** (projects shown used Loops & Threads Cozy Wool in Thunder [90 yds./82m])

- **2 skeins of super bulky yarn in oatmeal** (projects shown used Loops & Threads Cozy Wool in Mushroom [90 yds./82m])

gauge swatch:
Super Bulky Garter Stitch

This first gauge swatch will teach you how to cast on, knit and bind off. The three projects in this chapter rely on these skills, so don't skip this step! To make things easier, all three projects in this chapter are made with the same gauge, so you only have to knit one gauge swatch for all three projects. Keep your gauge swatches when you're finished—they make great mug mats!

materials

• Super bulky yarn (such as Loops & Threads Cozy Wool or Lion Brand Wool-Ease Thick & Quick)

• Size US 10 (6mm) needles, or size needed to obtain gauge

• Measuring tape

• Scissors

• Yarn needle

gauge

11 stitches × 26 rows = 4" (10.2cm) square

Left-handed Knitters

Some lefties are able to learn knitting the standard way. If you are one of those fortunate lefties, I strongly recommend that you follow the instructions as written. It will make your future in knitting so much easier.

If you're unable to knit without reversing the movements, you're still in luck. The patterns in this book will work no matter how you knit them.

For this swatch, you'll want to use the actual yarn you plan on using for your project. The projects shown in this chapter are made with Loops & Threads Cozy Wool, a super-bulky yarn. Lion Brand Wool-Ease Thick & Quick is another popular super-bulky yarn that will give you similar results.

I used size 10 (6mm) needles to knit these projects, so start with size 10 (6mm), but be aware you might need to change your needle size to get the right gauge. Don't worry, I'll explain this once you've made your swatch.

CAST ON

The very first step of knitting a gauge swatch is casting on. All the projects in this book use the same cast-on method: the long-tail method. If you've learned a different method, feel free to use it. It won't make a noticeable difference to the finished projects.

It's important to cast on loosely because if your cast-on is too tight you won't be able to get your needle through the loops when knitting. This will cause you frustration. If you're having trouble with your cast-on tension, cast on with a larger knitting needle or hold two needles together.

1. Find the end of your yarn; if you're working from a skein (as shown), pull the end from the center and wrap any extra around the outside of the skein.

2. Leave yourself a tail at least 24" (61cm) long.

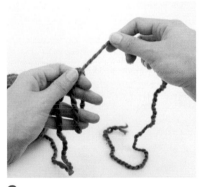

3. Drape the loose end of the yarn over your left hand, pinch it in place with your thumb and wrap the yarn around your fingers. Bring the yarn back up to your thumb and pinch it, making a loop.

4. Still pinching the ends together with your thumb and forefinger, slip the loop off your fingers.

5. With your right hand, grab the end that hangs down behind the loop (the loose end) and pull it through the loop, creating a second loop.

6. Let go with your left hand and pull the end attached to the ball until the knot is tight.

7. Slide the loop onto a knitting needle. The loose end should be in front, closest to you. The end connected to the ball should be in the back. Pull the loose end to tighten the loop around the knitting needle. Don't pull too tight—you need to be able to slide a knitting needle through the loop later when you knit the stitch. The slipknot, your first stitch, is now complete.

8. Hold the needle with the slipknot in your right hand and the pointed end of the needle facing your left hand. Slide the thumb and forefinger of your left hand between the two ends hanging off the needle. Wrap your other fingers around the yarn hanging below and spread your thumb and forefinger, creating a diamond shape with the yarn.

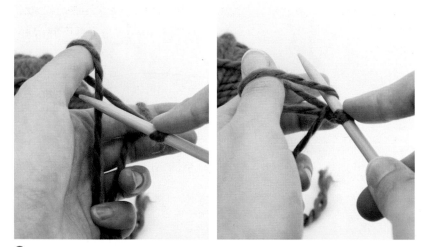

9. Move the knitting needle in your right hand toward your body. This will create a loop of yarn around your thumb. Slide the knitting needle through the loop, keeping the yarn wrapped around your thumb.

10. Move the knitting needle over to your forefinger and pull the yarn that's wrapped over your forefinger onto the knitting needle and through the loop on your thumb.

11. Drop the loop from your thumb. Gently pull on both ends to tighten the stitch. Again, don't pull too tightly—you need to be able to knit into these stitches.

12. Repeat steps 8 through 12 until there are 11 stitches on your needle. Remember, the slipknot you created counts as a stitch.

KNIT

Now that you've cast on, it's time to actually start knitting! The first row is always the hardest, so hang in there. If you're having trouble getting your needle into the stitches, you may have cast on too tightly. Not to worry. Simply pull the cast-on stitches off your needle and pull a loose end to unravel the stitches. Cast on again, but do it looser this time (practice makes perfect!). You can also use a larger needle or hold two needles together to make sure your cast-on stitches are loose enough.

There are a few things to keep in mind while knitting. First, the stitches you're *going* to knit are always on the left-hand needle, and the stitches you've *just* knit will be on the right-hand needle. Also, try to be conscious of how tightly you're pulling the yarn. Don't knit like you're angry at the yarn, but also avoid being so laid back that your stitches fall right off the needle. Relax and have fun. The more you do it, the easier it will get.

13. Hold the needle with your stitches in your left hand. Push the stitches forward on the needle so that they're close to the tip.

14. Hold the empty needle in your right hand. Slip your right needle through the loop of the first stitch. Move from the left side on the front of the stitch through to the right side on the back of the stitch. The two knitting needles will form an *X*.

15. Use your left hand to hold the two knitting needles in place, pinching them where they cross. With your right hand, grab the yarn end that's still attached to the ball. Double-check that you've grabbed the correct end—you won't get very far if you start knitting with the short end. Wrap the yarn around the back of the right-hand needle and pull it down between the two needles.

16. Continue to hold the yarn in your right hand, pinching it between your thumb and forefinger. At the same time, use your remaining fingers to grab hold of the right knitting needle. Slide the right needle down, under the left needle and through to the front, creating a new loop on your right needle.

17. Use the right needle to slide the stitch off the left needle. You now have 1 knit stitch on your right needle.

The loose tail end may slip up a bit between your stitches at this point. Just hold it down and in place for the time being. Once you start your next stitch, it will stay put.

18. Slide your right needle into the next stitch on the left needle and repeat the process: in, around, to the front, and off.

19. Continue knitting until you've knit all the stitches on the left needle. Count the stitches to make sure you still have 11.

20. Flip your work around, moving the needle that's holding stitches to your left hand again and the empty needle to your right. Continue knitting in each stitch and switching your needles at the end of each row until your swatch measures 4" (10.2cm) from the cast-on edge.

BIND OFF

At the end of every project, you will need to bind off. It's fairly straightforward, but once again, you'll want to pay attention to how tightly or loosely you're knitting. If you bind off too tightly, the finished edge will also be tight and will pull in. If it's too loose, the edge may ruffle a bit. If you found yourself knitting tightly throughout the gauge swatch, you may want to swap your right-hand needle for a larger one as you bind off to keep from knitting too tightly.

21. Begin the next row, as usual, but knit only 2 stitches.

22. Slip your left needle through the first stitch on your right needle, from left to right.

23. Pull the first stitch on the right needle over the second stitch and slip it off the left needle. You now have 1 stitch on the right needle.

24. Knit another stitch so there are, again, 2 stitches on the right-hand needle.

25. Use your left needle to slip the first stitch over the second stitch on the right needle and then slip it off the left needle.

26. Continue in this fashion, knitting 1 stitch so that there 2 stitches on the right needle, then slipping the first stitch over the second, until you have no stitches left on the left needle and only 1 stitch on the right.

27. Cut the yarn, leaving a short tail (about 6" [15.2cm]).

28. Pull your needle straight up, pulling the yarn through the stitch.

MEASURING A GAUGE SWATCH

It's time to measure and see how close you are to the gauge needed for this chapter's projects.

1. Lay the gauge swatch on a flat surface and place your tape measure vertically over the gauge swatch. Count how many rows make up 4" (10.2cm). Each garter stitch ridge is equal to 2 rows. For these projects, you want about 26 rows to equal 4" (10.2cm), although the row gauge won't be as important as the stitch gauge.

2. Measure your 11-stitch width (this is your stitch gauge). Lay your measuring tape across the swatch; if it measures 4" (10.2cm), your gauge is perfect! Congrats!

If your swatch measures more than 4" (10.2cm), your gauge is too loose (your stitches are too big!). You need to go down to a smaller needle size. If the swatch measures less than 4" (10.2cm), your gauge is too tight; knit another swatch with larger needles.

NEXT STEPS

So, your garter stitch gauge swatch is complete. Now what? If your gauge matches the gauge called for in these projects, you're ready to start your first project. If your gauge doesn't match, you may want to knit another swatch with different needles. If your swatch measures less than 4" (10.2cm), your gauge is too tight and you need to go up a needle size. If your gauge swatch measures more than 4" (10.2cm), your gauge is too loose; go down a needle size. If your gauge was close, but not quite, don't worry about it. These projects are pretty forgiving, so you'll still get great results, even if you're off by ¼" (6mm).

What do you do with this knit square? Use it! Weave in the ends and you've made a coaster. Or, if you'd rather use the yarn for something else, frog it (the official knitting term for ripping out a project).

WEAVE IN THE ENDS

1. Thread one end onto a tapestry needle. Pull it up through the stitches, catching the backs of the stitches. Stitch up and down the piece until the end is woven in. Repeat with the second end.

2. Trim both ends close to the swatch, being careful not to cut your knitting.

Another Way to Knit

Another method of knitting is called continental knitting or picking. The end result is the same, but the way you hold your yarn is slightly different. This method can be a little harder to get the hang of, but theoretically, it is a faster way to knit because you don't have to let go with one hand and wrap the yarn around the needle. Instead, you hold the yarn in your left hand and pick it with your right needle as you go through the stitch.

1. Hold the yarn in your left hand, bringing it under the needle and up over your index finger.

2. Slide your right needle through the first stitch, front to back, and slide the needle under the yarn draped over your index finger.

3. Pull the yarn through the stitch.

4. Slide the stitch off the left needle. You have knit 1 stitch.

5. Repeat steps 1–4 to knit the entire row.

Garter Stitch Hat

This hat is the perfect first project. It requires very little knitting (much less than a scarf!) and can be worn multiple ways (fold up that brim!). If you've never made a pom-pom before, don't worry. It's even easier to make than the hat.

materials

- 2 skeins of super bulky yarn in a main color (project shown uses Loops & Threads Cozy Wool in Mushroom [90 yds./82m])

- 1 skein of super bulky yarn in a contrast color (for the pom-pom) (project shown uses Loops & Threads Cozy Wool in Thunder [90 yds./82m])

- Size US 10 (6mm) knitting needles

- Tape measure

- Tapestry needle

- Scissors

- Pom-pom maker

gauge

11 stitches and 26 rows = 4" (10.2cm) square

finished size

17½" × 10" (44.5cm × 25.4cm), not including pom-pom. The width of the hat is adjustable.

Note

Feel free to use any yarn you'd like for the pom-pom, but be warned: pom-poms require a lot of yarn. I used the same yarn as the hat body, but in a contrasting color. I use this color again in the other projects later in the chapter.

I used Loops & Threads Cozy Wool for my projects, but you have other options. Lion Brand Wool-Ease Thick & Quick is carried in most major craft stores, and it's a great alternative. You can also go to your local yarn shop and ask for suggestions.

1. Determine your hat size. When you cast on for this hat, you're casting on the height of your hat, not the width. You'll knit until you reach the width needed for your head. To determine this, measure the circumference of your head. Since the hat will stretch, subtract 4" (10.2cm) from your circumference. Write down this number for later use.

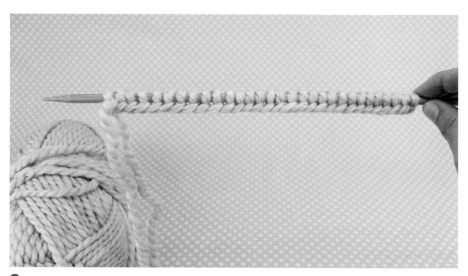

2. Leaving a 47" (1.2m) tail, cast on 30 stitches with the main color. If you need a refresher course, flip back to the gauge swatch directions at the beginning of the chapter.

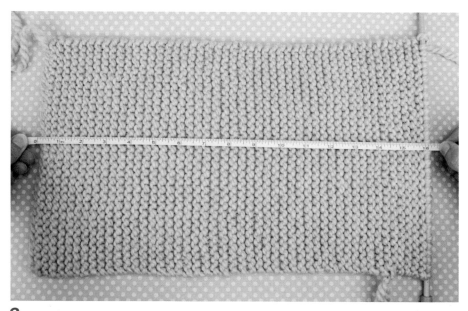

3. Begin knitting (remember, the first row is the hardest). Work in garter stitch (knit every row) until your hat measures your head circumference minus 4" (10.2cm). For me, this number is 17½" (44.5cm). There's a good chance you'll need to join a new ball before you reach this length. See Attaching a New Ball of Yarn, on the next page, for help.

4. Bind off the last row (refer to the garter stitch gauge swatch for detailed instructions).

5. Cut the yarn from the ball, leaving a 20" (50.8cm) tail.

6. Pull the yarn tail through the last stitch to finish the row.

Attaching a New Ball of Yarn

When you're getting near the end of your ball of yarn, you'll need to attach a new ball. The rule of thumb is that you need four times the length of your row to knit across. If you have less yarn than that, tie on a new ball.

1. Tie the new ball of yarn around the loose end with an overhand knot and slide it up so it's close to your needle.

2. Knit as usual, making sure you use the end attached to the new ball of yarn. When you finish your project, untie the knot and weave in the ends.

7. Use one of the loose yarn tails to sew up the side seam, or cut a new thread if your tails are too short (to show where the stitches go, I've used a contrasting yarn). Thread a tapestry needle and line up the long edges of your hat. Pull your needle through a stitch on one side, then through the stitch on the opposite side. Continue all the way up.

8. Thread your tapestry needle with the other yarn end (again, I've used a contrasting color so you can see where the stitches are).

9. Weave your needle in and out along the top edge of the hat (the edge where you joined the second ball of yarn), creating a running stitch.

10. Pull the yarn tight to cinch the top of the hat closed.

11. Take a few stitches across the top of the hat to help close up the top. The pom-pom will cover this end, so if it's not perfectly closed, you won't be able to tell.

12. Weave in your ends.

13. Make a pom-pom with your contrast yarn. Directions vary slightly between pom-pom makers, so follow the manufacturer's directions for your particular maker.

14. Trim your pom-pom into shape, but don't trim the yarn you tied around the pom-pom; leave these tails long. Warning: This gets messy.

15. Attach the pom-pom to the top of your hat. The easiest way to do this is to take the two long tails, thread them through the top of the hat to the inside and tie the ends together tightly.

16. Weave in the ends of the pom-pom, trim the ends, turn your hat right-side out, and you're done!

the pattern

- CO 30 sts in the MC.

- Work in garter stitch until the piece measures 17½" (44.5cm) (or the circumference of your head minus 4" [10.2cm]). BO.

- Fold the hat in half and seam together the CO and BO edges.

- Gather the top of the hat and stitch it closed.

- Create and sew on the pom-pom with the CC, if desired. Weave in the ends.

Color Block Scarf

Though long, the narrow rows and patches of color make this scarf
a fast knit. Experiment with the color to suit your style.

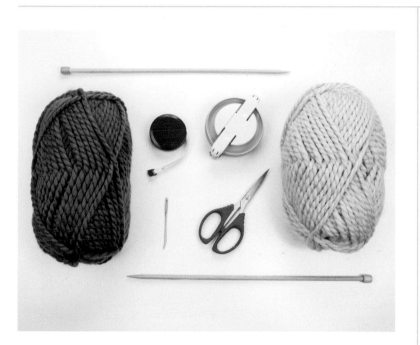

materials

- 1 skein super bulky yarn in a main color (project shown uses Loops & Threads Cozy Wool in Thunder [90 yds./82m])

- 1 skein super bulky yarn in a contrast color (project shown uses Loops & Threads Cozy Wool in Mushroom [90 yds./82m])

- Size US 10 (6mm) knitting needles

- Tape measure

- Tapestry needle

- Scissors

- Pom-pom maker

gauge

11 stitches and 26 rows = 4" (10.2cm) square

finished size

$3\frac{1}{4}$" × $58\frac{1}{2}$" (8.3cm × 148.6cm), not including pom-poms.

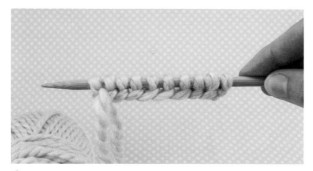

1. Leaving a 17" (43.2cm) tail, cast on 10 stitches with the contrast color. Refer to the garter swatch section if you need help.

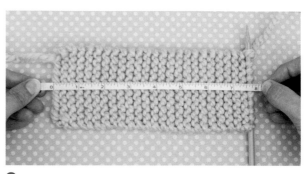

2. Knit every row until the piece measures 7½" (19.1cm) from the cast-on edge.

3. Cut the contrast color from the ball, leaving about a 6" (15.2cm) tail. Tie on the main color and begin knitting, making sure you're using the strand attached to the ball of yarn.

4. Knit until the main color section measures 47" (119.4cm). Feel free to adjust the length of your scarf. This length makes a scarf long enough to wrap around your neck and tie in a knot.

Tip

This section of knitting is long and can get tedious. Stop every few rows to count the stitches on your needle and make sure you haven't added or dropped any. It's easier to fix these mistakes if you catch them early. Flip to the Common Mistakes section at the back of the book if you need help correcting a mistake.

5. Change back to the contrast color. Make sure you join the yarn on the same edge you did previously (this will keep the front side of the scarf looking consistent). Again, leave 6" (15.2cm) tails on both yarns and begin knitting with the contrast color attached to the ball of yarn.

6. Continue knitting in garter stitch (knit every row) with the contrast color until the section measures 4" (10.2cm).

7. Bind off the stitches. When you get to the last stitch, cut a 6" (15.2cm) tail and pull the end through the last stitch.

8. Make 2 pom-poms from the contrast yarn; follow the manufacturer's instructions for your pom-pom maker. Trim them to an equal size but leave the strand that you tied around the center of each pom-pom long. You'll use these strands to attach the pom-poms to the scarf.

9. Use the yarn tail at the cast-on edge to sew a running stitch along the edge. (I've used a contrasting yarn so you can see the stitches.)

10. Pull tightly to gather the edge, then stitch through the end again to secure the stitches. Repeat with the bind-off edge.

11. Take a pom-pom and thread the first long tail through a gathered scarf end. Weave the tail along the edge. Do the same with the second long tail on the pom-pom, then weave both ends into the scarf on the back side and trim. Repeat this process with the second pom-pom on the other end of the scarf.

12. Undo the knots along the edge of the scarf where you changed colors. Weave the ends into the matching sections of color on the wrong side of the scarf (the side where the color changes don't make a clean line). If you weave them into a section of a different color, the ends will show. Trim the ends close to the scarf, being careful not to cut the scarf.

the pattern

- CO 10 sts in the CC.

- Work in garter stitch until the piece measures 7½" (19.1cm).

- Switch to the MC and work garter stitch for 47" (1.2m) from the CO. End with a WS row.

- Switch to the CC and work in garter stitch for 4" (10.2cm). BO.

- Make 2 pom-poms from the CC.

- Gather the ends and attach the pom-poms. Weave in the ends.

Garter Stitch Mitts

Sure, you have to knit two of these, but these mitts are very simple. Just leave a gap in the seam for your thumb, and you're good to go. Adjust the placement and size of the thumb hole to fit your hand comfortably.

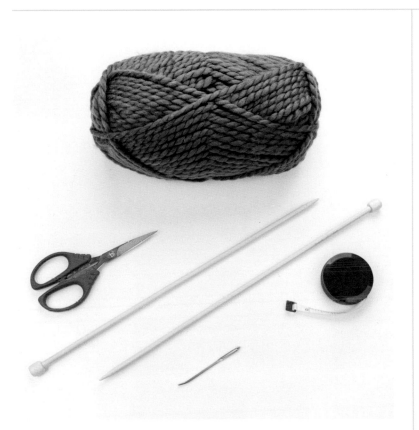

materials

- 1 skein super bulky yarn (project shown uses Loops & Threads Cozy Wool in Thunder [90 yds./82m])

- Size US 10 (6mm) knitting needles

- Tape measure

- Tapestry needle

- Scissors

gauge

11 stitches and 26 rows = 4" (10.2cm) square

finished size

6½" × 7" (16.5cm × 17.8cm)

1. Leaving a 32" (81.3cm) tail, cast on 20 stitches.

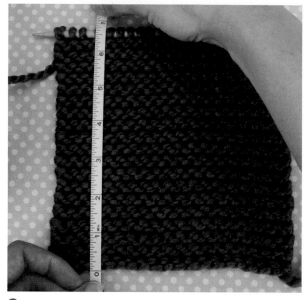

2. Knit until the piece measures 6½" (16.5cm) from the cast-on edge.

3. Bind off all the stitches. Cut the yarn, leaving a tail long enough to stitch up the sides.

4. Fold the piece in half, matching up the cast-on edge to the bind-off edge.

5. Use the tail to whipstitch up the side, as previously described in the *Garter Stitch Hat* project. (A contrasting yarn is used here to show the stitches.)

6. Stitch up the side for 4½" (11.4cm).

7. Make another stitch in the same place as your last to reinforce the thumb opening.

8. Run the needle and thread along one side of the mitt, winding through the stitches without connecting the sides.

9. Leave a 1" (2.5cm) opening for the thumb, then stitch the 2 sides together again, reinforcing the start of the seam with an extra stitch as in step 7.

10. Continue sewing up to the top of the piece, taking care to join the top 2 stitches on either side of the seam.

11. Weave in the ends.

12. Make a second mitt exactly the same as the first. There's no difference between the right and left.

the pattern

Make 2

- CO 20 sts.

- Work in garter stitch for 6½" (16.5cm). BO.

- Fold in half with the CO and BO edges together. Seam up, leaving a 1" (2.5cm) opening for your thumb. Weave in the ends.

stockinette stitch

When you think of knit garments, you're probably thinking of stockinette stitch. It's one of the most recognizable stitch patterns out there. It does require that you learn a second stitch, the purl stitch, but trust me—it's worth learning.

The projects in this chapter build on what you've already learned, combining sections of garter stitch with stockinette stitch.

FOR THESE PROJECTS

If you plan on knitting all the projects in this chapter, you need the following:

- **1 skein of medium yarn in gray** (projects shown used Lion Brand Wool-Ease in Oxford Gray [197 yds./180m])

- **1 skein of medium yarn in dark yellow** (projects shown used Lion Brand Wool-Ease in Mustard [197 yds./180m])

gauge swatch:
Worsted Stockinette Stitch

This gauge swatch uses slightly smaller yarn and needles than those used in the first chapter. The knitting itself will feel slightly less dense. To knit this gauge swatch, you should already know how to cast on, knit and bind off. Refer back to the Garter Stitch Gauge Swatch if you need help with any of these techniques. This gauge swatch will teach you how to purl and how to use alternating rows of knitting and purling to make stockinette stitch.

materials

- Medium yarn (such as Lion Brand Wool-Ease)
- Size US 8 (5mm) needles, or size needed to obtain gauge
- Measuring tape
- Scissors
- Yarn needle

gauge

18 stitches × 24 rows = 4" (10.2cm) square

Knit your swatch using the yarn you intend to use for your project. These projects all use medium-weight yarn, a very common yarn weight. If you can't find Lion Brand Wool-Ease or want to use something else, you should have no trouble finding something similar. I prefer yarn that isn't 100% acrylic (Wool-Ease has some wool in it), but choose whatever feels right to you.

CAST ON

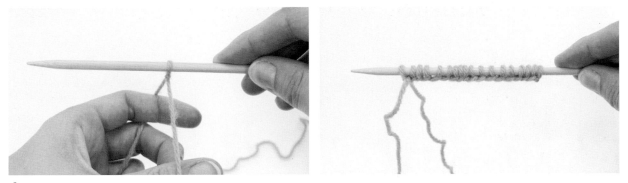

1. Leaving a 25" (63.5cm) tail, cast on 18 stitches. Refer to the Garter Stitch Gauge Swatch if you need help.

PURL

2. Holding the needle with the cast-on stitches in your left hand and the empty needle in your right, slide the right-hand needle into the first stitch, going from right to left through the front of the stitch.

3. Hold both needles in place with your left hand, and grab the yarn attached to the ball with your right hand.

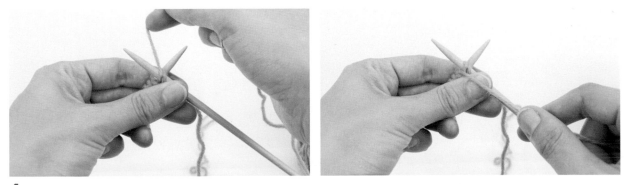

4. Wrap the yarn counterclockwise around the right-hand needle (the needle closest to you).

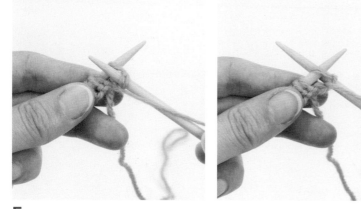

5. Pull the right needle down the front of the left needle and up around the back of the left-hand needle.

6. Slide the stitch off the left needle. This first stitch can be a little awkward; hold the loose tail end in place with your left hand to keep it from sliding up between the stitches.

7. Repeat the process for the next stitch. Slide your right needle into the front of the next stitch, from right to left, wrap the yarn counterclockwise around the right needle, slide the right needle behind the left needle and pull the stitch onto the right needle.

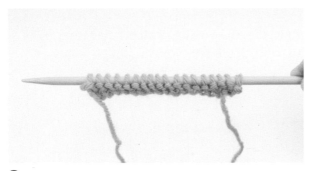

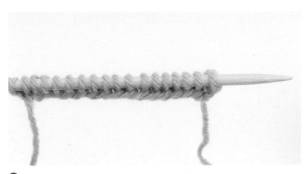

8. Continue purling across the row until all stitches are on the right-hand needle. Look closely at these stitches. Note how there are bumps instead of flat stitches along the row you just finished. This is the wrong side (or back side) of your work.

9. Turn the needle around, placing it in your left hand. This is the right side (or front) of your work.

10. Knit across all the stitches in the row. Again, the side with the smooth *V* stitches is the right side of your work.

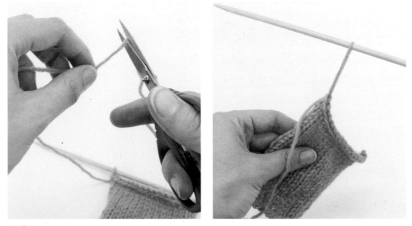

11. Continue alternating purl and knit rows (purl on the bumpy side, knit on the smooth side) until your swatch measures 4" (10.2cm). End with a purl row so that your bind-off row will be a knit row.

12. Bind off all the stitches, knitting them as you go. Refer to the Garter Stitch Gauge Swatch if you need help. When you have one stitch left, cut the yarn leaving a 6" (15.2cm) tail and pull the tail through the last stitch.

MEASURING A GAUGE SWATCH

Stockinette stitch can be difficult to measure because the edges tend to roll. To help get a more accurate measurement for your gauge swatch, pin down the edges of the swatch, being careful not to stretch the piece too much.

1. Lay your tape measure over the swatch, top to bottom. It should measure just about 4" (10.2cm). Count how many rows are in 4" (10.2cm) by counting the number of *V*s in one column. This is your row gauge.

2. Since you've already cast on the number of stitches called for in the gauge measurement, you only need to measure to get your stitch gauge. If the swatch measures 4" (10.2cm) from side to side, your gauge is right on. If your swatch measures more than 4" (10.2cm), your gauge is too big and you need to go down a needle size. If your swatch measures less than 4" (10.2cm), your gauge is too small and you need to go up a needle size.

NEXT STEPS

Once you have the correct gauge, you're ready to start the projects in this chapter. Your gauge swatch can be used as a mug mat or coaster, but as I've mentioned, the edges of stockinette stitch don't like to lie flat. Once you're done measuring your gauge swatch, steam it gently with an iron while the edges are pinned down. Let the swatch dry with the edges pinned. This will help the swatch lie flat.

Another Way to Purl

Just as there is an alternate way to knit, there's an alternate way to purl, also referred to as continental style. As with continental knitting, the yarn is picked from your left hand instead of wrapped with your right.

1. Hold the yarn on the front side of your left needle and drape it up over your index finger

2. Slide your right needle through the first stitch as you would to purl.

3. Move the right needle under the yarn on your index finger.

4. Bring your index finger down, wrapping the yarn around the right needle.

5. Keeping your index finger down, pull the yarn through the stitch, to the back of the work.

6. Pull the stitch off of the left needle and reset your fingers to repeat steps 1–5.

Turban Headband

Keep your ears warm and looking stylish with this simple stockinette stitch headband. The garter stitch accent cleverly hides the seam while adding a bit of a turban feel.

materials

- 1 skein medium yarn in a main color (project shown uses Lion Brand Wool-Ease in Oxford Gray [197 yds./180m])

- 1 skein medium yarn in a contrast color (project shown uses Lion Brand Wool-Ease in Mustard [197 yds./180m])

- Size US 8 (5mm) knitting needles

- Tape measure

- Tapestry needle

- Scissors

gauge

18 stitches and 24 rows – 4" (10.2cm) square

finished size

18½" × 4½" (47cm × 11.4cm). The length of the headband is adjustable.

Note

I used Lion Brand Wool-Ease for this project. If you choose to use it as well, know that it comes in a variety of weights; make sure you're buying the right one. Any medium-weight yarn will work for this project, but I recommend looking for one that has a bit of wool in it instead of one that is 100% acrylic. The wool will make your headband a little warmer.

1. Determine your headband size. Measure the circumference of your head. Since the headband will stretch a bit, subtract 3" (7.6cm) from your circumference. Write this number down for later use. For me, this number is 18½" (47cm). The following instructions have been written for that measurement, so adjust your length as needed.

2. Leaving a 26" (66cm) tail, cast on 20 stitches with the main color. If you need a refresher course, flip back to the Garter Stitch Gauge Swatch tutorial.

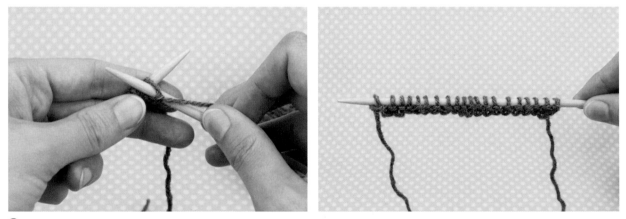

3. Purl the first row. This is the wrong side (or back) of your headband.

4. Knit the next row. This is the right side (or front) of your headband.

5. Continue working in stockinette stitch, alternating rows of purl stitches and knit stitches, until the headband measures the needed length, in this case 18½" (47cm). End with a purl row.

Do I Knit or Purl?

If you can't remember whether you're supposed to knit or purl a row, just look at the stitches. Knit the side with smooth *V* stitches and purl the side with raised, bumpy stitches.

KNIT

PURL

6. Your next row will be a knit row. Bind off all stitches, leaving a 12" (30.5cm) tail. Pull the tail through the last stitch.

7. Leaving a 6" (15.2m) tail, cast on 7 stitches with the contrast color.

8. Work in garter stitch (knit every row) until the piece measures 2½" (6.4cm).

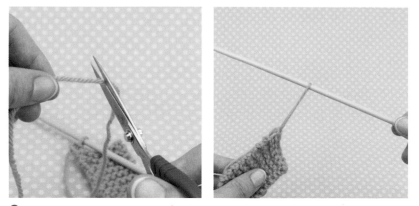

9. Bind off all the stitches. When you get to the last stitch, cut the yarn, leaving a 6" (15.2cm) tail. Pull the tail through the last stitch.

10. Wrap the garter stitch band around your main headband piece.

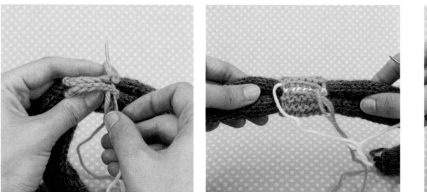

11. Sew the cast-on and bind-off edges of the garter stitch band together using one of the yarn tails. (I've used a contrasting color so you can see the stitches.)

12. Fold the main headband piece in half, right sides (smooth sides) together.

13. Sew up the cast-on and bind-off edges of the headband, working your needle through corresponding stitches on each side using one of the main color yarn tails (I have used a constrasting color to show the stitches).

14. Slide the garter stitch band over the seam in the headband, then twist the band so that the seam is on the back side.

the pattern

- CO 20 sts in the MC.

- Work in stockinette stitch until the piece
  measures the circumference of your head
  minus 3" (7.6cm).

- BO the sts and sew up the CO and BO edges.

- CO 7 sts with the CC.

- Work in garter stitch for 2½" (6.4cm).

- BO. Wrap the piece around the headband
  and sew the ends together.

- Slide the band over the headband seam.
  Weave in the ends.

Banded Gaiter

This gaiter has a somewhat snug fit, sort of like a cozy turtleneck.
Be careful pulling it on; it may muss up your do.

materials

- 1 skein medium yarn in a main color (project shown uses Lion Brand Wool-Ease in Oxford Gray [197 yds./ [180m])

- 1 skein medium yarn in a contrast color (project shown uses Lion Brand Wool-Ease in Mustard [197 yds./180m])

- Size US 8 (5mm) knitting needles

- Tape measure

- Tapestry needle

- Scissors

gauge

18 stitches and 24 rows = 4" (10.2cm) square

finished size

19" × 8" (48.3cm × 20.3cm)

Tip

These rows are long. Really long. If you can help it, try to avoid stopping in the middle of a row. Stitches tend to slide off the needles when you stop in the middle. When you're done with a row and ready to put your knitting away, push the stitches away from the pointed end of your needle.

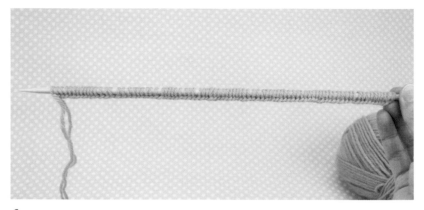

1. Leaving a 100" (2.5m) tail, cast on 84 stitches with the contrast color.

2. Knit in garter stitch (knit every row) for about 1" (2.5cm).

3. Cut the contrast color, leaving a 6" (15.2cm) tail and tie on the main color.

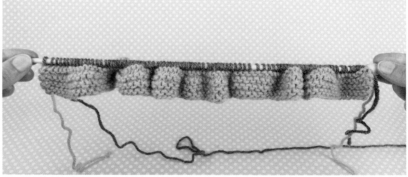

4. Knit across the first row. This is the right side of your cowl.

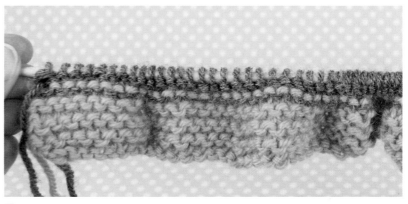

5. Purl the next row. This is the wrong side of your work. Notice how the bumps are on this side of the cowl.

6. Continue working in stockinette stitch (alternating knit and purl rows) until the cowl measures about 7" (17.8cm) from the cast-on edge.

7. Cut the main color, leaving a 6" (15.2cm) tail. Tie on the contrast color.

Tip

Make sure you have the same number of contrast color rows at either end of your gaiter by counting the ridges. There are 4 ridges of the contrast color on the bottom edge, so knit until there are 4 ridges at the top (8 rows total).

8. Knit for 1" (2.5cm) in garter stitch (knit every row).

9. Bind off all the stitches, knitting as you go until there is only 1 stitch left on the needle. Cut the yarn, leaving a 12" (30.5cm) tail, then pull the yarn through the last stitch.

10. Fold the gaiter in half, right sides together, and seam up the edges (I used a contrasting yarn so you can see the stitches). If you want the seam to be invisible, switch to your main color when seaming the middle section.

11. Weave in the ends and turn the gaiter right side out.

the pattern

- CO 84 sts in the CC.

- Work in garter stitch until the piece measures 1" (2.5cm).

- Switch to the MC and work in stockinette stitch for 7" (17.8cm) from the CO. End with a WS row.

- Switch to the CC and work in garter stitch for 1" (2.5cm).

- BO all sts and sew up the sides. Weave in the ends.

Cuffed Stockinette Mitts

These mitts are worked in a similar way to the *Garter Stitch Mitts*, but the addition of contrasting cuffs gives them a little extra punch. Again, the mitts are seamed up the side, leaving an opening for your thumb.

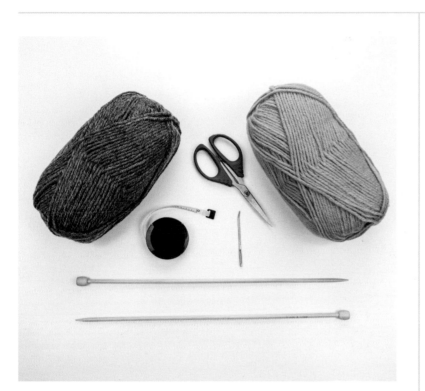

materials

- 1 skein medium yarn in a main color (project shown uses Lion Brand Wool-Ease in Oxford Gray [197 yds./180m])

- 1 skein medium yarn in a contrast color (project shown uses Lion Brand Wool-Ease in Mustard [197 yds./180m])

- Size US 8 (5mm) knitting needles

- Tape measure

- Tapestry needle

- Scissors

gauge

18 stitches and 24 rows = 4" (10.2cm) square

finished size

3½" × 6" (8.9cm × 15.2cm)

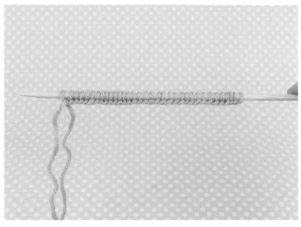

1. Leaving a 48" (1.2m) tail, cast on 34 stitches with the contrast color.

2. Knit in garter stitch (knit every row) until the piece measures 2" (5.1cm).

3. Cut the contrast color, leaving a 6" (15.2cm) tail, and tie on the main color.

4. Knit across all the stitches in the main color. This is now the right side of your work.

5. Purl all the stitches in the next row. This is the wrong side of your work (notice how there are bumps on this side—that's how you know it's the wrong side).

6. Continue working in stockinette stitch (alternating rows of knit and purl) until the stockinette section measures 3½" (8.9cm). Make sure the next row you knit will be a right-side row. If it's not, purl 1 more wrong side row.

7. Cut the main color, leaving a 6" (15.2cm) tail, and tie on the contrast color.

8. Knit 5 rows of garter stitch (knit every row). If you lose track of the rows, count the ridges. You should have 2 distinct ridges on the front of your work and the last row you knit will be a wrong-side row.

9. Bind off all the stitches, knitting as you go. Cut the yarn, leaving a 12" (30.5cm) tail, and pull the tail through the stitch.

10. Fold the mitt in half, right sides together.

11. Stitch up the side of the mitt using 1 of the loose ends (I've used a constrasting yarn so you can see the stitches). Stop after 2½" (6.4cm). Make an extra stitch here to secure the bottom of the thumb opening.

12. Work the yarn up 1 side of the thumb opening, catching just the edge of the stitches. The thumb opening should be about 1" (2.5cm).

13. Join both sides together again, making an extra stitch to secure the top of the thumb opening, and sew up to the top of the mitt.

14. Weave in the ends.

15. Knit a second mitt the same as the first.

the pattern

Make 2

- CO 34 sts in the CC.

- Work in garter stitch until the piece measures 2" (5.1cm).

- Switch to the MC and work in stockinette stitch for $3\frac{1}{2}$" (8.9cm). End with a WS row.

- Switch to the CC and work 5 rows of garter stitch. BO.

- Fold the mitt in half and sew the sides together, leaving a 1" (2.5cm) gap for your thumb. Weave in the ends.

3
ribbing

All of the projects in this chapter are knit in ribbing. Ribbing is another classic look (think fisherman's caps). It has a lot of stretch, which is great for hats and boot cuffs, but less useful for scarves. Practice your blocking skills on your gauge swatch to transform it into a mug mat, then take on a bigger project and block the scarf to reveal the details of the ribbing pattern.

FOR THESE PROJECTS

If you plan on knitting all the projects in this chapter, you need the following:

- **2 skeins of bulky yarn** (projects shown used Lion Brand Alpine Wool in Olive [92 yds./84m])

- **2 skeins of bulky yarn** (projects shown used Lion Brand Alpine Wool in Oatmeal [92 yds./84m])

gauge swatch:
Bulky 2×2 Ribbing

You already know all of the stitches you need to make ribbing (knit and purl). Now you just need to use different stitches in the same row. No big deal.

materials

- Bulky yarn (such as Lion Brand Alpine Wool)

- Size US 9 (5.5mm) needles, or size needed to obtain gauge

- Measuring tape

- Scissors

- Yarn needle

gauge

16 stitches × 20 rows = 4" (10.2cm) square

Use the actual yarn you plan on using for your project. The projects shown in this chapter are made with Lion Brand Alpine Wool, a bulky yarn made from 100% wool, but you can use any yarn of the same size and fiber content. I used size US 9 (5.5mm) needles to knit these projects; start with size 9 (5.5mm), but be aware that you might need to change your needle size to get the right gauge.

CAST ON

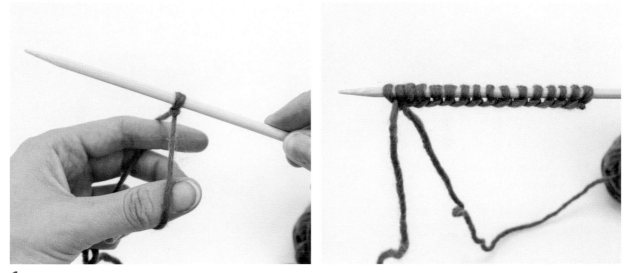

1. Leaving a 27" (68.6cm) tail, cast on 16 stitches.

FIRST RIBBING ROW

2. Knit the first 2 stitches.

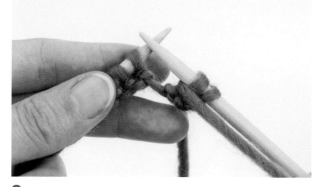

3. Pull the yarn from the back to the front, going under the right-hand needle (make sure you don't wrap the yarn over the needle). Once the yarn is in the front, purl 2 stitches.

4. Bring the yarn around to the back, again going under the right-hand needle, not over. Knit 2 stitches.

5. Continue working across the row, working in the established pattern (knit 2 stitches, purl 2 stitches). The row will end with 2 purl stitches.

6. Begin the next row by knitting 2 stitches (if you're not sure whether you should knit or purl the stitches, look at the stitches on your needle. If they're smooth, knit them).

7. Purl the next 2 stitches and continue working your way across the row, knitting 2 stitches and purling 2 stitches. Your stitches should all line up: knit the smooth stitches and purl the bumps. If your 2 × 2 pattern gets off, you can try fixing it. See the Common Mistakes section at the back of the book for help.

8. Continue knitting in the established pattern (knit 2 stitches, purl 2 stitches across every row) until your swatch measures about 4" (10.2cm).

9. To retain the rib pattern when binding off, begin as you normally would by knitting 2 stitches. Pass the first stitch on the right needle over the second and off the needle. The next stitch on your left needle is a purl stitch. Purl that stitch so that you again have 2 stitches on your left needle. Pull the first stitch over the second. Continue working 1 stitch from your right needle (look at the stitch to see whether you should knit or purl it), and binding off 1 stitch when you have 2 stitches on your right needle.

10. When you just have 1 stitch left on your right needle, cut the yarn, leaving a 6" (15.2cm) tail. Use your needle to pull the tail up through the final stitch.

MEASURING A GAUGE SWATCH

Ribbing can be tricky to measure. To determine the gauge, you need to know whether the ribbing should be measured stretched or unstretched. We'll be measuring the swatch stretched. You'll want to stretch the ribbing slightly (not as far as it will go, but enough that you can see the purl stitches between the knit stitches) and pin the sides down.

1. For good measure, count how many rows make up 4" (10.2cm). Since these patterns generally tell you to knit until your piece is a specific measurement, not a certain number of rows, you don't need to worry if your row gauge is off.

2. Measure across your 16 stitches (remember to measure with the ribbing slightly stretched). If your swatch is less than 4" (10.2cm) wide, your stitches are too small and you need to go up a needle size. If your swatch is bigger than 4" (10.2cm), your stitches are too large and you need to go down a needle size.

NEXT STEPS

Because ribbing is so stretchy, it's a pretty forgiving stitch. If your gauge is close, go ahead and proceed with the projects. If you'd like to use your swatch as a mug mat, it's a good idea to block it, much like you did the stockinette stitch swatch. Spray your yarn with cold water to make it damp and pin it into a square. Let it dry completely before removing the pins. Weave in the ends, and you're ready to use your mug mat.

Watchman's Cap

Wear this classic hat two ways: with the brim folded up for a snug fisherman's-style cap, or with the brim unfolded for a looser, slouchier fit.

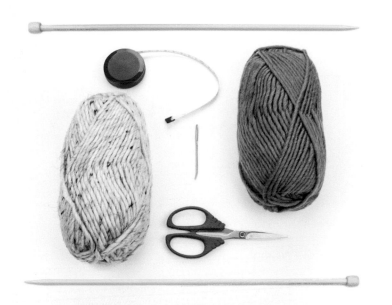

materials

- 1 skein bulky yarn in a main color (project shown uses Lion Brand Alpine Wool in Oatmeal [92 yds./85m])

- 1 skein bulky yarn in a contrast color (project shown uses Lion Brand Alpine Wool in Olive [92 yds./85m])

- Size US 9 (5.5mm) knitting needles

- Tape measure

- Tapestry needle

- Scissors

gauge

16 stitches and 20 rows = 4" (10.2cm) square, unstretched

finished size

18" × 7½" (45.7cm × 19.1cm) with brim folded

This hat stretches a lot, so one size fits most (from 17"–24" [43.2cm–61cm]). If your head circumference doesn't fit in that range, adjust the number of stitches you cast on. Add or subtract in groups of 4 so your rows always start with knit 2 and end with purl 2, and your ribbing will continue uninterrupted.

Note

This project is made with 100% wool, which can be a little scratchy on sensitive skin. If possible, feel this yarn before committing to it. It has a great natural look and is extremely warm, but it may not be the right yarn for everyone. A softer, but more expensive, alternative would be a yarn made of 100% merino wool.

IMPORTANT: Projects made of wool must be hand washed in cold water. If you clean them in the washing machine or use hot water, you will likely felt your project, which will shrink it and change the texture of the knitting.

1. Leaving a 108" (2.7m) tail, cast on 64 stitches (or the number of stitches you need for a custom-fit hat) with the main color. If you need a refresher course, flip back to the Garter Stitch Gauge Swatch tutorial.

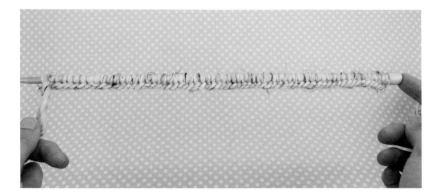

2. Work across the first row in a 2 × 2 rib pattern: Knit 2 stitches, then purl 2 stitches. Continue in this pattern across the row, ending with 2 purl stitches.

3. Work the second row the same way you did the first: Knit 2 stitches, purl 2 stitches all the way across. Continue working the established rib pattern until your hat measures 1¼" (3.2cm).

4. Switch colors, tying on your contrast color. Leave the main color attached. Do not cut.

5. Knit 2 rows of garter stitch (knit every stitch) with the contrast color, then cut the yarn, leaving a 6" (15.2cm) tail.

6. Pick up the main color that's still attached to your hat and use it to work in 2 × 2 ribbing (knit 2 stitches, purl 2 stitches) across the row.

7. Continue working in the rib pattern (knit 2, purl 2) until the hat measures 9" (22.9cm) from the cast-on edge.

Note

This hat will likely use almost your entire ball of yarn. If you run out of yarn before you reach 9" (22.9cm), it's okay. Your hat will just be a little shorter. Alternatively, you can add another stripe of the contrast color to make up the length. Just make sure you have at least 12" (30.5cm) of yarn left to finish the hat.

8. Cut the yarn, leaving at least a 12" (30.5cm) tail. Thread the yarn through the tapestry needle, and slide the tapestry needle through all the stitches on your needle, from left to right. (No need to bind off!)

9. Slide the stitches off the needle and pull the yarn tight, gathering the stitches in a closed circle.

10. Make a few stitches across the center of the circle to help anchor it closed.

11. Fold the hat in half and sew up the seam. Use the tail from the cast-on edge if it's long enough (or a new piece if it's not). I've used a contrasting color so you can see where I've placed the stitches. Use the main color for a seam that is less visible.

12. Weave in the ends at the top of the hat and trim them close to the hat. (Leave the ends toward the bottom for the next step.)

13. Weave in the ends around the brim on the other side of the hat so, when the hat is right-side out and the brim is folded up, the ends won't show.

Note

If you plan on folding up the brim of your hat, make sure you seam up the hat on the side shown.

the pattern

- CO 64 sts in the MC.

- Work in 2 × 2 ribbing for 1¼" (3.2cm).

- Switch to the CC and knit 2 rows.

- Switch to the MC and knit 1 row.

- Work in 2 × 2 ribbing until hat measures 9" (22.9cm) from CO.

- Thread the yarn through the stitches to gather the top. Sew up the side seam. Weave in the ends.

Fringed Scarf

The ribbed pattern in this scarf alternates in the middle, creating a striking visual. Add some fringe to give it a retro vibe.

materials

- 2 skeins bulky yarn in a main color (project shown uses Lion Brand Alpine Wool in Olive [92 yds./84m])

- 1 skein bulky yarn in a contrast color (project shown uses Lion Brand Alpine Wool in Oatmeal (92 yds./84m])

- Size US 9 (5.5mm) knitting needles

- Tape measure

- Tapestry needle

- Scissors

- 4" (10.2cm) square of cardboard

gauge

16 stitches and 20 rows = 4" (10.2cm) square

finished size

6" × 50" (15.2cm × 127cm), not including fringe.

Note

This scarf benefits greatly from blocking, especially if you use 100% wool yarn to knit it. When you finish knitting the scarf, soak it thoroughly in cold water. Gently squeeze out the excess water, then lay the scarf out on a towel and stretch it into the desired dimensions. Pin the edges down as you go so the scarf will keep its shape as it dries. Let the scarf dry completely before you unpin it. This process is called blocking.

If at some point you need to wash your scarf, hand wash it in cold water (or follow the directions on your yarn label). Lay it flat to dry. You may need to pin it down while it dries to ensure the ribbing doesn't scrunch up.

1. Leaving a 42" (1.1m) tail, cast on 26 stitches with the main color. Refer back to the Garter Stitch Gauge Swatch if you need help.

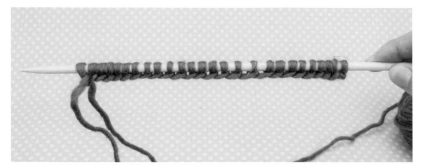

2. Begin working in 2 × 2 rib pattern (knit 2 stitches, purl 2 stitches). You will begin and end with 2 knit stitches. The next row will begin and end with 2 purl stitches. Continue working in this pattern until the scarf measures 4¼" (10.8cm).

3. Tie on your contrast color, leaving a 6" (15.2cm) tail. Do not cut the main color yarn; you'll use it again shortly.

4. Work 2 rows of garter stitch (knit every stitch) using your contrast color. Cut the contrast color, leaving a 6" (15.2cm) tail. (This is the front of your scarf.)

5. Pick up the main color you left attached to the scarf. Knit every stitch for 1 row. (This will give you a clean line between the color changes.)

6. Your next row is a wrong side row. Here you will reverse the ribbing pattern you established in the first section. If the first 2 stitches of the ribbing below are bumps, start this section with knits, and vice versa. Continue working in this pattern until the scarf measures 37" (94cm) from the color change.

Tip

Can't remember if you should be knitting or purling? Look at the next stitch on your needle. If it's smooth, knit it. If it's bumpy, purl it.

Don't worry if you don't reverse the ribbing in the middle section of the scarf; it will look good even if you continue in the same pattern for the entire length of the scarf.

7. Make sure your next row is a right-side row; if it's not, work 1 more row. Tie on the contrast color (but don't cut the main color).

8. With the contrast color, work 2 rows of garter stitch (knit every row). Cut the contrast color, leaving a 6" (15.2cm) tail.

9. Pick up your main color (which should still be attached to the scarf) and knit 1 row. Again, this will give you a clean line on the right side of your scarf where the color changes.

10. Begin working in 2 × 2 rib. Reverse the rib pattern that you used in the middle section of the scarf. Repeat the pattern from the first section. Alternate these 2 rows for 4¼" (10.8cm)

Tip

The idea is for both end sections to be the same length. You'll get close by just measuring, but if you want to be extra accurate, count the number of rows in both sections and adjust the section you're working on accordingly.

11. Bind off all the stitches, working in the established rib pattern. When you have 1 stitch left, leave about 6" (15.2cm), cut the yarn and pull it through the last stitch.

12. Untie the knots along the edges where you changed colors and weave in the ends on the wrong side of the scarf (shown). Weave in the ends along the cast on and bind off edges as well.

13. To make the fringe, wrap the contrasting yarn around the cardboard 52 times (this will give you enough strands to make all the fringe).

14. Cut the yarn along 1 end of the cardboard. You should have 52 pieces of yarn.

15. Fold 1 strand in half, and thread the folded part through your needle. Pull the loop of yarn partially through the bottom of the scarf.

16. Pull the cut ends of the yarn through the loop and pull to tighten the loop around the scarf.

17. Continue adding fringe, 1 piece for each stitch along each edge of the scarf. Trim the fringe to even it out, if necessary.

the pattern

- CO 26 sts in the MC.

- Work in Ribbing A (start with a WS row) for 4¼" (10.8cm).

- Switch to the CC and knit 2 rows (the first row is a RS row).

- Switch to the MC and knit 1 row (RS).

- Work Ribbing B (start with a WS row) until the scarf measures 37" (94cm).

- Switch to the CC and knit 2 rows.

- Switch to the MC and knit 1 row.

- Work in Ribbing A (start with RS row) for 4¼" (10.8cm).

- BO all sts. Weave in the ends. Add fringe if desired.

RIBBING A

- (RS): *P2, K2; repeat from * until last 2 sts, P2

- (WS): *K2, P2; repeat from * until last 2 sts, K2

RIBBING B

- (RS): *K2, P2; repeat from * until last 2 sts, K2

- (WS): *P2, K2; repeat from * until last 2 sts, P2

Ribbed Boot Cuffs

Have you ever seen those faux turtlenecks or collars? The ones you wear under your sweater to give the illusion of a full shirt underneath? I've never understood those. But boot cuffs make sense. They give the illusion of cozy, handknit socks without the hassle of stuffing thick socks into tight boots. Basically, they're like dickies for your ankles.

materials

- 1 skein bulky yarn in a main color (project shown uses Lion Brand Alpine Wool in Oatmeal [90 yds./85m])

- 1 skein bulky yarn in a contrast color (project shown uses Lion Brand Alpine Wool in Olive [90 yds./85m])

- Size US 9 (5.5mm) knitting needles

- Tape measure

- Tapestry needle

- Scissors

gauge

16 stitches and 20 rows = 4" (10.2cm) square

finished dimensions

9" × 4¾" (22.9cm × 12.1cm), measured at the widest point.

Note

These boot cuffs are designed for wearing under ankle boots, not knee-high boots. Depending on the size of your leg, you may be able to pull them up higher. To make a wider boot cuff, just cast on more stitches in groups of 2 (to account for the rib pattern). Every 2 stitches added should add ½" (1.3cm) to the width of your cuff.

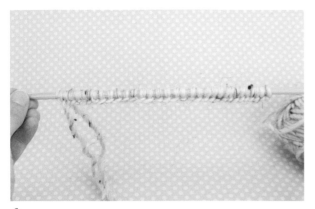

1. Leaving a 56" (1.4m) tail, cast on 32 stitches with the main color.

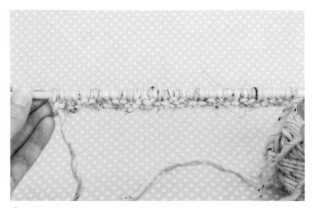

2. Work across the first row in 2 × 2 ribbing (knit 2 stitches, purl 2 stitches).

3. Continue knitting in the 2 × 2 rib pattern until the cuff measures 2½" (6.4cm) from the cast-on edge.

4. Tie on your contrast color, but do not cut the main color.

5. Using the contrast color, knit 2 rows in garter stitch (knit every stitch).

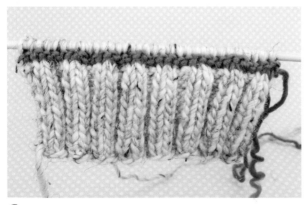

6. Pick up the main color (still attached) and knit 1 row (knit every stitch). Leave the contrast color attached; you'll use it again. (This is the right side of your cuff.)

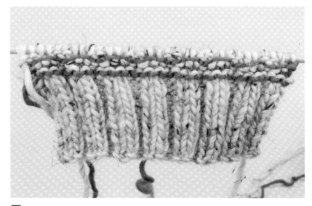

7. Knit the next row in 2 × 2 rib pattern (knit 2, purl 2). (This is the wrong side of your cuff.)

8. Pick up the contrast color and knit 2 rows in garter stitch (knit every stitch). Cut the contrast color, leaving a 6" (15.2cm) tail.

9. Knit 1 row (knit every stitch) with your main color, then work 3 rows in rib pattern (knit 2, purl 2). Your next row should be a right-side row.

10. Bind off all the stitches, keeping the rib pattern as you go. When there's 1 stitch left on the needle, cut the yarn, leaving a 12" (30.5cm) tail. Pull the tail through the last stitch.

11. Fold the cuff in half, right-sides together, matching up the sides.

12. Take one of the loose ends (preferably the main color) and stitch up the sides (I used a contrasting yarn so you can see the stitches).

13. Untie the knots along the edge and weave in the ends.

14. Knit a second cuff the same as the first.

the pattern

- CO 32 sts in the MC.

- Work in 2 × 2 ribbing for 2½" (6.4cm).

- Switch to the CC and knit 2 rows.

- Switch to the MC and knit 1 row.

- Work 1 row in 2 × 2 ribbing.

- Switch to the CC and knit 2 rows.

- Switch to the MC and knit 1 row.

- Work 3 rows in 2 × 2 ribbing.

- BO all sts and sew up the sides. Weave in the ends.

4

seed stitch

Seed stitch looks complicated, but it's really quite simple. The only thing you need to remember is to knit the purls and purl the knits. This will make more sense once you work up your gauge swatch. You'll also use 1 × 1 ribbing in some of these projects. No worries; it's exactly the same as 2 × 2 ribbing, except you knit one stitch, purl one stitch instead of knit two stitches, purl two stitches.

FOR THESE PROJECTS

If you plan on knitting all the projects in this chapter, you need the following:

- **1 skein of bulky yarn in lavender** (projects shown used Bernat Alpaca Chunky in Lavender [120 yds./110m])

- **1 skein of bulky yarn in tan** (projects shown used Bernat Alpaca Chunky in Wheat [120 yds./110m])

- **2 skeins of bulky yarn in violet** (projects shown used Lion's Brand Lion's Pride Woolspun in Orchid [127 yds./116m])

gauge swatch:
Bulky Seed Stitch

The projects in this chapter call for two different types of yarn (in three colors total), both bulky, but one is a little fluffier and lighter. It's fine to use the same type of yarn for all three colors, but if you do use the yarns suggested, use the lighter, fluffier yarn to knit your gauge swatch.

materials

- Bulky yarn (such as Bernat Alpaca)
- Size US 10 (6mm) needles, or size needed to obtain gauge
- Measuring tape
- Scissors
- Yarn needle

gauge

16 stitches × 21 rows = 4" (10.2cm) square

Use the actual yarn you plan on using for your project. The projects shown in this chapter use two different fibers: alpaca and wool. The alpaca yarn is used for the main body of the projects where the gauge matters most (the headband and the bootcuffs), so use it to test your gauge. The wool yarn used in these projects is the same weight but may give you a slightly larger gauge.

CAST ON

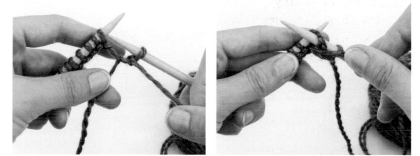

1. Leaving a 25" (63.5cm) tail, cast on 13 stitches. Refer to the Garter Stitch Gauge Swatch if you need help.

FIRST ROW

2. Knit the first stitch.

3. Bring the yarn around to the front of the needle (going under the right needle) and purl the next stitch.

4. Move the yarn to the back again, and knit the next stitch.

5. Continue working across the row, alternating purl and knit stitches, ending with a knit stitch.

6. Look at the first stitch on your needle before you start the next row. When working in seed stitch, remember to knit the purl stitches and purl the knits. The first stitch has a bump (it's a purl stitch), so you knit it.

7. Bring the yarn around to the front. You'll notice that the next stitch is smooth (a knit stitch), so purl it.

8. Continue working across the row, alternating knit and purl stitches. If you forget whether you should knit or purl the next stitch, just remember to do the opposite of what you did on the previous row. If the next stitch has a bump in the front, knit it. If the stitch is smooth, purl it.

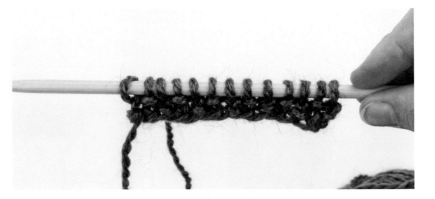

9. Continue working in the seed stitch pattern until your swatch measures 4" (10.2cm).

10. To bind off, keep working the stitches in pattern. Knit the first stitch and purl the second. Pass the first stitch on your right needle over the second and off the needle.

11. Knit the next stitch so there are 2 stitches on the right needle. Pass the stitch on the right over the stitch on the left and off the needle.

12. Continue across the row, alternating knit and purl stitches, and passing the right stitch over the left every time there are 2 stitches on your right needle. When you have only 1 stitch left on your right needle, cut the yarn, leaving a 6" (15.2cm) tail. Pull the yarn through the last stitch.

MEASURING A GAUGE SWATCH

Unlike ribbing, seed stitch lays flat, so there's no need to pin it before measuring your gauge. Counting rows and stitches is easy on seed stitch: Every other stitch is a bump.

1. Since you knit until your swatch was 4" (10.2cm), it should be pretty close to that length (your bind off row may have added a bit). Lay your tape measure over the swatch and count how many rows make up 4" (10.2cm).

2. Measure across the width of your swatch to see if it equals 4" (10.2cm). If it does, your gauge is all set. If your swatch measures less than 4" (10.2cm), you'll need to go up a needle size. If your swatch measures more than 4" (10.2cm), you'll need to go down a needle size.

NEXT STEPS

As with all the projects in this book, the gauge isn't especially crucial, though it's good practice to get your gauge right. If your row gauge is off, there's no need to knit another swatch. If your stitch gauge is off by more than just a little (say an ¼" [6mm]), knit another swatch, going up a needle size if your swatch measured less than 4" (10.2cm) and down a needle size if your swatch measured more than 4" (10.2cm).

Once your swatch is the correct size, weave in the ends, and you have yourself a mug mat. Enjoy!

Classic Headband

Perfect for hitting the slopes or the ski lodge, this headband offers just the right amount of warmth and style.

materials

- 1 skein bulky yarn in a main color (project shown uses Bernat Alpaca Chunky in Wheat [120 yds./110m])

- 1 skein bulky yarn in a contrast color (project shown uses Lion Brand Lion's Pride Woolspun in Orchid [127 yds./116m])

- Size US 10 (6mm) knitting needles

- Tape measure

- Tapestry needle

- Scissors

gauge

13 stitches and 21 rows = 4" (10.2cm) square

finished size

17" × 3" (43.2cm × 7.6cm)

This headband will fit a head 17"–22" (43.2cm–55.9cm). If you need to make it bigger or smaller, cast on more or fewer stitches in groups of 2.

1. Leaving a 108" (2.7m) tail, cast on 56 stitches (or the number of stitches you need for a custom-fit headband) with the contrast color. If you need a refresher course, flip back to the Garter Stitch Gauge Swatch tutorial.

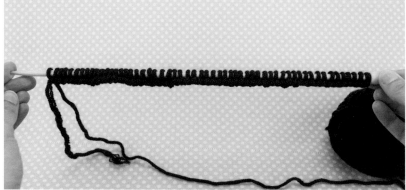

2. Work across the first row in a 1 × 1 rib pattern (knit 1 stitch, purl 1 stitch all the way across).

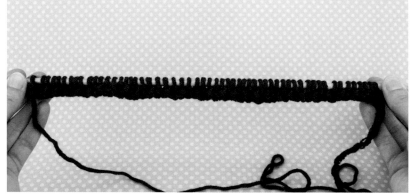

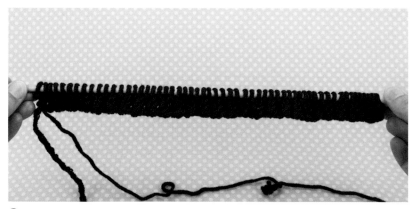

3. Work 2 more rows of 1 × 1 rib (to do this, make sure to knit the knit stitches and purl the purl stitches—the opposite of what you do to make seed stitch).

4. Cut the contrast color, leaving a 6" (15.2cm) tail. Tie on the main color.

5. Using the main color, begin working in seed stitch. You'll want to do the opposite of the rib pattern you established. Start the row with a purl stitch and work your way across, alternating knit and purl stitches.

6. Start the next row with a knit stitch and work your way across in the seed stitch pattern (knit 1 stitch, purl 1 stitch). Continue working in seed stitch until your headband measures 2½" (6.4cm) from the cast on edge.

7. Cut the main color, leaving a 6" (15.2cm) tail, and tie on the contrast color.

8. Using the contrast color, begin knitting in 1 × 1 rib pattern. This first row will essentially be a continuation of the seed stitch pattern. Depending on which row you end with, you'll start with either a knit or purl stitch. Just make sure it's the opposite of the stitch below it.

9. Work 2 more rows in 1 × 1 ribbing (match the knit stitches to the knit stitches in the previous row and the purl stitches to the purl stitches).

10. Bind off the stitches, keeping the rib pattern in place. When you have 1 stitch left, cut the yarn, leaving a 12" (30.5cm) tail and pull it through the last stitch.

11. Fold the headband in half, matching up the sides. Use one of the tails to sew up the sides (I've used a constrasting color so you can see the stitches).

12. Untie the knots where you changed colors and weave in the ends.

the pattern

- CO 56 sts in the CC.

- Work 3 rows in 1 × 1 ribbing.

- Switch to the MC and work in seed stitch until the piece measures 2½" (6.4cm) from CO edge.

- Switch to the CC and work 3 rows in 1 × 1 ribbing.

- BO all sts and sew up the sides. Weave in the ends.

Wrap Around Cowl

This nubby cowl is long enough to wrap snuggly under your chin, but it looks just as good worn hanging long. Or be extra daring and pull it over your head hood style. Options!

materials

- 2 skeins bulky yarn in a main color (project shown uses Lion Brand Lion's Pride Woolspun in Orchid [127 yds. [116m])

- 1 skein bulky yarn in contrast color A (project shown uses Bernat Chunky Alpaca in Lavender [120 yds./110m])

- 1 skein bulky yarn in contrast color B (project shown uses Bernat Chunky Alpaca in Wheat [120 yds./110m])

- Size US 10 (6mm) knitting needles

- Tape measure

- Tapestry needle

- Scissors

gauge

13 stitches and 21 rows = 4" (10.2cm) square

finished size

8½" × 23¾" (21.6cm × 60.3cm). The length of the cowl is taken while the cowl is lying flat.

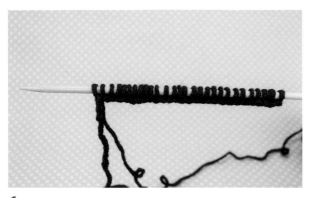

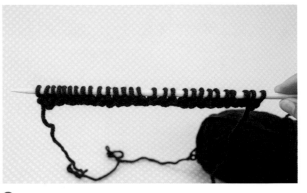

1. Leaving a 53" (1.3m) tail, cast on 28 stitches with the main color. Refer back to the Garter Stitch Gauge Swatch if you need help.

2. Begin the seed stitch pattern. Knit 1 stitch, purl 1 stitch across the first row, alternating each stitch.

3. Start the second row with purl 1 stitch, knit 1, alternating each stitch for the entire row. Continue working in the established seed stitch pattern (knit the purl stitches and purl the knits) until the cowl measures 35" (88.9cm). (You'll likely need to tie on a second ball of the main color at some point.)

4. Cut the main color, leaving a 6" (15.2cm) tail and tie on contrast color A.

5. Work in the seed stitch pattern using contrast color A for 4" (10.2cm).

6. Cut contrast color A, leaving a 6" (15.2cm) tail, and tie on contrast color B.

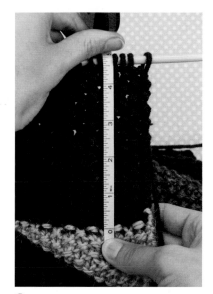

7. Using contrast color B, work in seed stitch pattern for 4" (10.2cm).

8. Cut contrast color B, leaving a 6" (15.2cm) tail and tie on the main color.

9. Using the main color, work 4½" (11.4cm) in seed stitch.

10. Bind off the stitches, maintaining the seed stitch pattern. When 1 stitch remains, cut the yarn, leaving a 12" (30.5cm) tail. Pull the tail through the stitch.

11. Fold the cowl in half, lining up the bind-off and cast-on edges.

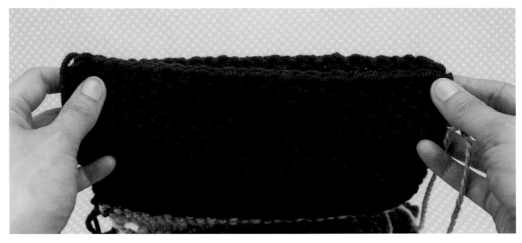

12. Use 1 of the main color loose ends to stitch up the seam. (I've used a contrasting color so you can see the stitches.)

13. Untie the knots where you changed colors and weave in all of the loose ends. Take care to weave in the ends in the same color sections—it will help your ends blend in.

the pattern

- CO 28 sts in the MC.

- Work in seed stitch for 35" (88.9cm).

- Switch to CC A and work in seed stitch for 4" (10.2cm).

- Switch to CC B and work in seed stitch for 4" (10.2cm).

- Switch to the MC and work in seed stitch for 4½" (11.4cm).

- BO all sts and sew the edges together. Weave in the ends.

Textured Boot Cuffs

These boot cuffs are a little larger, intended to be worn peeking out of the top of your tall boots. Feel free to adjust the length if you prefer your cuffs a bit slouchier. The optional braided drawstring helps to keep your cuffs in place.

materials

- 1 skein bulky yarn in a main color (project shown uses Bernat Alpaca Chunky in Wheat [120 yds./110m])

- 1 skein bulky yarn in contrast color A (project shown uses Bernat Alpaca Chunky in Lavender [120 yds./110m])

- Small amount of scrap yarn for braided ties in contrast color B (project shown uses Lion's Brand Lion's Pride Woolspun in Orchard)

- Size US 10 (6mm) knitting needles

- Tape measure

- Tapestry needle

- Scissors

gauge

13 stitches and 21 rows = 4" (10.2cm) square

finished size

13" × 5¾" (33cm × 14.6cm). The cuff is measured at the widest point.

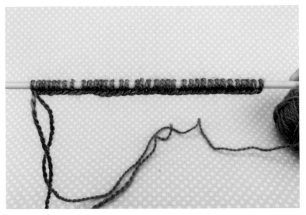

1. Leaving an 87" (2.2m) tail, cast on 46 stitches with the contrast color.

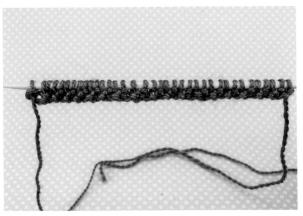

2. Work across the first row in 1 × 1 ribbing (knit 1, purl 1 all the way across).

3. Continue working in 1 × 1 ribbing (knit the knit stitches, purl the purl stitches) until the cuff measures 2" (5.1cm) from the cast-on edge.

4. Cut the contrast color, leaving a 6" (15.2cm) tail, and tie on the main color.

5. Work across the row in seed stitch with the main color (knit the purl stitches and purl the knit stitches). You'll start with a purl stitch and end with a knit stitch.

6. Continue working in seed stitch (knit the purls, purl the knits) for 3" (7.6cm).

7. Cut the main color, leaving a 6" (15.2cm) tail, and tie on the contrast color.

8. Begin working in 1 × 1 ribbing. Ideally, you don't want the ribbing to match up with the stitches below. If the first stitch you're working into is a knit stitch (as it is in the photo), purl it.

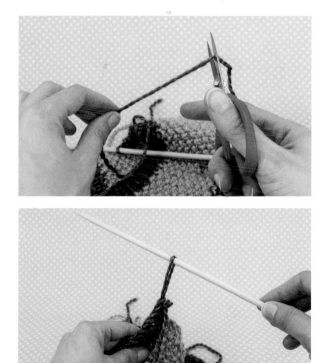

9. Work in 1 × 1 ribbing for 4 rows (in the ribbing section, make sure you knit the knit stitches and purl the purl stitches, the opposite of what you did in the seed stitch section).

10. Bind off the stitches, working in the rib pattern, until 1 stitch remains. Cut the yarn, leaving a 12" (30.5cm) tail; pull the tail through the stitch.

11. Fold the cuff in half, matching up the sides.

12. Stitch up the sides, using 1 of the long tails (I've used a contrasting color here so you can see the stitches).

13. Untie the knots along the edge and weave in the loose ends. Make a second cuff the same as the first.

14. Using the scrap yarn, cut 3 strands about 40" (1m) long. Braid the strands. Repeat to make a second braid.

15. Weave the braid around the top of your cuff and tie it at the back. Repeat with the second cuff.

the pattern

Make 2

- CO 46 sts in CC A.

- Work in 1 × 1 ribbing for 2" (5.1cm).

- Switch to the MC and work in seed stitch for 3" (7.6cm).

- Switch to CC A and work 4 rows of 1 × 1 ribbing.

- BO all sts and sew the sides together.

- Make a braid using CC B and weave it into the top ribbing of the cuff. Weave in the ends.

Common Mistakes

It's inevitable that you will make mistakes when knitting. Don't sweat it. Part of the charm of a handmade item is that it's handmade, not made by a machine. Embrace the flaws in your projects; they're what make your projects unique. That being said, I'm a perfectionist and am always more likely to rip out several weeks worth of knitting than to live with a mistake. If you're like me, use this section to fix or avoid common mistakes.

The easiest way to fix a mistake is just to rip out the knitting and start over (called frogging). I recommend this for beginners because it gives you more practice knitting and because some of the methods used to fix mistakes can be a little confusing.

FROGGING
(HOW TO RIP OUT KNITTING)

Frogging can be a little scary. The concept behind it is that you slide all the stitches off your needle and pull on the yarn. Your knitting unravels, and you can quickly pull out a few rows, or however much you need to get to the point before your mistake occurred.

1. Slide all the stitches off the needle and pull on the yarn to unravel the stitches.

2. Stop unraveling at a point before your mistake happened. Finish unraveling to the end of the row, then slide your needle through the stitches, making sure you start with the stitches at the end of the row, not the beginning (where the yarn is attached).

FIXING BACKWARD STITCHES

If you find yourself ripping out stitches or fixing mistakes, you may end up putting the stitches back on the needle the wrong way. It's an easy fix.

Just slide the stitch off the needle and put it on the right way.

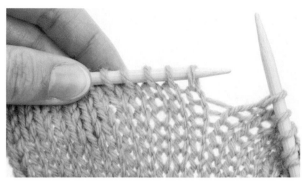

The first stitch on the left needle in both photos is backwards. Notice that the back of the loop sticks out farther to the right than the front of the loop. Slide the stitch off the needle and turn it so that the part of the loop that was at the back is now at the front.

TAKING OUT ONE STITCH AT A TIME

Sometimes you catch your mistakes early on (while you're still on the same row). If so, there's no need to take everything off the needle. Instead, just unknit the stitches one at a time.

1. With your left needle, reach into the loop below the first stitch on your right needle.

2. Slide that loop onto your left needle and pull the right needle out. Pull on the yarn to unravel the stitch. You've undone 1 stitch.

DROPPED STITCH

Sometimes a stitch may fall off your needle (especially if you're prone to stopping midrow). If left to its own devices, the stitch will unravel and work its way down. If you've dropped a stitch, you'll either need to fix it using the method below or frog your knitting to the point of the dropped stitch.

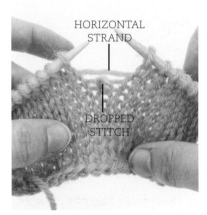

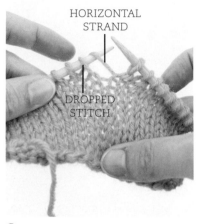

1. This is a dropped stitch. The loop sticking out between the needles has come unraveled. To fix this, knit across the row until the dropped stitch is between your needles.

2. Slide your left needle through the dropped stitch from left to right and under the horizontal strand of yarn.

3. Use your right needle to pull the dropped stitch over the horizontal strand and off the needle. The stitch is now on your left needle, ready to be knit with the rest of the row.

To fix a dropped stitch on the purl side, slide your right needle from right to left, through the stitch and under the horizontal bar. Use your left needle to pull the stitch over the horizontal bar and off the needle. Slip the stitch from your right needle to the left so that it can be purled with the rest of the row. This method also can be used to save a stitch that's dropped down several rows. Just keep working the stitch through the horizontal bars until it's all the way back up to the top.

UNFINISHED STITCH

An unfinished stitch is created when you wrap the yarn around to knit or purl, but you don't actually work the yarn through the stitch. Both the wrapped yarn and the original stitch end up on the needle. If you knit both of these separately, you'll end up with too many stitches on your needle and, very likely, a hole in your work. Fortunately, as you work across the next row, it's pretty obvious if you've done this, and it's relatively easy to fix.

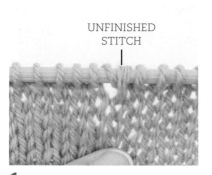

UNFINISHED STITCH

1. This is what an unfinished stitch looks like after you've finished your knit row

2. Purl the next row until you get to the unfinished stitch.

3. Drop the first loop off the needle. You now have a dropped stitch situation. Slide the next stitch (the unfinished stitch) on your left needle to the right needle, and slide the right needle under the horizontal bar. Pull the stitch over the bar and off your right needle.

KNITTING TWICE INTO THE FIRST STITCH

One of the most common mistakes beginning knitters make is to knit twice into the first stitch. Pay attention to where your yarn is before you start a row, and you should be able to avoid this mistake.

If you do knit into the stitch, fix it by either frogging several rows until you, once again, have the correct number of stitches, or work back, undoing one stitch at a time.

In this photo, the yarn is in the wrong place to start the row. It's pulled up over the needle, which in turn pulls up the bottom of the first stitch, making it look like 2 stitches.

This is where your yarn should be to start a row: straight down. There's only 1 loop to knit through.

STOPPING IN THE MIDDLE OF A ROW

I don't recommend putting down your knitting midrow, but sometimes it can't be avoided. In addition to making sure you haven't lost any stitches, you also need to make sure you're knitting in the right direction when you pick your project back up. You don't want to turn around and knit back the way you came halfway through a row.

If you're not sure where to start when you pick up your work, remember that once you've started a row, your yarn will always be on the right needle. In this photo, you should knit to complete the row.

This photo shows what it would look like if you tried to work in the other direction. The yarn is on the left needle, meaning those are the stitches that have already been worked. You need to turn this around so that the needle with the yarn attached is in your right hand.

SPLITTING STITCHES

One last thing to watch for when you're knitting is splitting your stitches. Some yarns are especially prone to splitting, so be careful and make sure you're sliding your needle all the way through a stitch. If a specific yarn is giving you a lot of trouble, I recommend ditching it and finding a yarn that won't separate so easily.

A split stitch won't ruin your project, and I don't think it's worth pulling your knitting out to fix the stitch. It does look a little sloppy, though, so just be careful as you work.

SPLIT STITCH

This is a split stitch. Notice how the needle is going through only some of the yarn.

Index

A

acrylic yarns, 8

B

Banded Gaiter, 57–61

binding off, 18–19

blocking process, 75, 83

boot cuffs

    Ribbed Boot Cuffs, 89–93

    Textured Boot Cuffs, 115–119

C

casting on, 13–15

Classic Headband, 103–107

Color Block Scarf, 31–35

continental knitting, 21, 49

cowls

    Banded Gaiter, 57–61

    Wrap Around Cowl, 109–113

Cuffed Stockinette Mitts, 63–67

F

Fringed Scarf, 83–87

frogging, 120

G

garter stitch, 11, 12–19

Garter Stitch Hat, 23–29

Garter Stitch Mitts, 37–41

gauge swatches, 6

    garter stitch, 12–19, 20

    ribbing, 70–74, 75

    seed stitch, 96–99, 100, 101

    stockinette stitch, 44–47, 48

H

hats

    Garter Stitch Hat, 23–29

    Watchman's Cap, 77–81

headbands

    Classic Headband, 103–107

    Turban Headband, 51–55

K

knit stitches, 15–17, 21

knitting needles, 9

L

left-handed knitters, 12

M

mistakes

    added stitches, 32

    backward stitches, 121

    dropped stitches, 32, 122

    knitting twice into first stitch, 123

    removing one stitch at a time, 121

    ripping out knitting (frogging), 120

    splitting stitches, 124

    stopping midrow, 58, 124

    unfinished stitches, 123

mitts

    Cuffed Stockinette Mitts, 63–67

    Garter Stitch Mitts, 37–41

P

patterns, 6

picking, 21, 49

pom-poms, 9, 23, 28

purl stitch, 45–47, 49

R

Ribbed Boot Cuffs, 89–93

ribbing, 69, 70–74

S

scarves

    Color Block Scarf, 31–35

    Fringed Scarf, 83–87

scissors, 9

seed stitch, 94, 96–99

stockinette stitch, 42, 44–47, 48

T

tape measure, 9

tension, 13, 15, 18

Textured Boot Cuffs, 115–119

tips

    counting rows, 59, 85

    counting stitches, 32

    forgetting if knit or purl, 53, 85

    weaving in ends, 20

Turban Headband, 51–55

W

Watchman's Cap, 77–81

wool, 8, 51, 77

Wrap Around Cowl, 109–113

Y

yarn

    attaching a new ball, 25

    choosing, 8

    weight, 8

yarn needles, 9

This book is dedicated to the knitting fairy (aka my mom).

ACKNOWLEDGMENTS

You may think that, with a little book like this, there couldn't possibly be many people to thank. You would be wrong. And in case this is the only book I ever write, I'm going to thank *everyone*.

First up, my parents. Thank you guys for being incredibly supportive of everything I do. Dad, thank you for graciously handing the phone over to Mom every time I call with a knitting question. Mom, thank you for fielding all my knitting questions.

To my sisters, thanks for always seeming pumped about the endless knitted gifts you've received over the years. There are more knitted gifts in your futures.

Thank you to my niece, Natalie White, for making my world a happier place.

Annie, thank you for being beautiful (inside *and* out, duh).

Thank you to my BFF Catherine for always giving honest, thoughtful feedback.

Thank you to F+W for giving me this opportunity, and special thanks to the team that made this book happen: Vanessa, Noel and Julie. I'm lucky I get to work with such a talented bunch every day.

Thank you to everyone who has listened to me talk about this book. I talk about this book a lot.

If you're reading this, maybe you've bought this book. In which case, thank you for that. I hope knitting will make you as happy as it makes me.

And finally, Mark. You are so talented at so very many things. This book is only the tip of the iceberg. Thank you for being my photographer, my life mate, my everything. We make a pretty great team.

ABOUT THE AUTHOR

Stephanie likes to ride horses. And knit. She works as a craft editor, which is every bit as much fun as it sounds. She lives in Cincinnati with a really dreamy dude and an adorable Labradoodle.

You Can Knit! Copyright © 2015 by Stephanie White. Manufactured in China. All rights reserved. No part of this book may be reproduced in any form or by any electronic or mechanical means including information storage and retrieval systems without permission in writing from the publisher, except by a reviewer who may quote brief passages in a review. Published by Fons & Porter Books, an imprint of F+W, a Content + eCommerce Company, 10151 Carver Rd, Ste. 200, Blue Ash, OH 45242. (800) 289-0963. First Edition.

fw

a content + ecommerce company

www.fwcommunity.com

19 18 17 16 15   5 4 3 2 1

DISTRIBUTED IN CANADA BY FRASER DIRECT
100 Armstrong Avenue
Georgetown, ON, Canada L7G 5S4
Tel: (905) 877-4411

DISTRIBUTED IN THE U.K. AND EUROPE BY F+W MEDIA INTERNATIONAL
Brunel House, Newton Abbot, Devon, TQ12 4PU, England
Tel: (+44) 1626 323200, Fax: (+44) 1626 323319
Email: postmaster@davidandcharles.co.uk

DISTRIBUTED IN AUSTRALIA BY CAPRICORN LINK
P.O. Box 704, S. Windsor NSW, 2756 Australia
Tel: (02) 4560-1600, Fax (02) 4577-5288
Email: books@capricornlink.com.au

ISBN-13: 978-1-4402-4396-7
SRN: T6437

EDITOR: Noel Rivera
DESIGNER: Julie Barnett
PHOTOGRAPHER: Mark Kleinfelder
PRODUCTION COORDINATOR: Jennifer Bass

General Knitting Information

In the instructions for the projects, I have favored US knitting terms. Refer to this box for the UK equivalents.

US Term	UK Term
bind off	cast off
gauge	tension
stockinette stitch	stocking stitch
reverse stockinette stitch	reverse stocking stitch
seed stitch	moss stitch
moss stitch	double moss stitch

Knitting Needle Sizes

US	METRIC	US	METRIC
0	2mm	10	6mm
1	2.25mm	10½	6.5mm
1½	2.5mm		7mm
2	2.75mm		7.5mm
2½	3mm	11	8mm
3	3.25mm	13	9mm
4	3.5mm	15	10mm
5	3.75mm	17	12.75mm
6	4mm	19	15mm
7	4.5mm	35	19mm
8	5mm	36	20mm
9	5.5mm		

Metric Conversion Chart

TO CONVERT	TO	MULTIPLY BY
inches	centimeters	2.54
centimeters	inches	0.4
feet	centimeters	30.5
centimeters	feet	0.03
yards	meters	0.9
meters	yards	1.1

Projects have been designed and created using imperial measurements and, although metric measurements have been provided, it is important to stick to using either imperial or metric throughout as discrepancies can occur.

More great knitting guides!

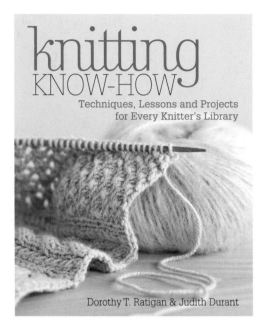

Knitting Know-How

by Dorothy T. Ratigan & Judith Durant

Knitting Know-How isn't just another collection of knitting techniques—it's an indispensable resource for making every stitch better! From basic knit and purl stitches to cables, lace, color knitting and garment design, you'll learn the ins and outs of improving your knitting and choosing one technique over another for the results you want. If you have ever wondered which cast-ons are suitable for socks, why you should always (always!) knit a gauge swatch, or how to fix a mis-crossed cable, this book is for you!

ISBN: 9781440218194

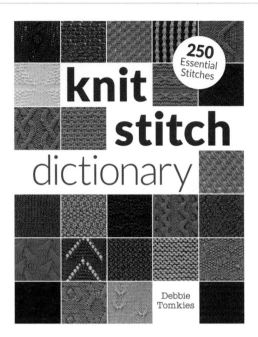

Knit Stitch Dictionary

by Debbie Tomkies

Every knitter needs a good stitch dictionary, and this volume is perfect for new and experienced knitters alike. *Knit Stitch Dictionary* offers 250 knit stitches, from simple knit-purl combos to fancy textured, color and lace stitch patterns. Knowing that not every knitter works in the same way, this indispensible guide has both written and charted instructions that clearly explain how to knit each stitch. A photo glossary at the back of the book offers a candy-box view of all the stitch patterns, allowing you to instantly choose the ones that strike your fancy.

ISBN: 9781620338841

Try our other great knitting books, magazines
and downloads at **knittingdaily.com**.